Cue Cards

FAMOUS WOMEN OF THE TWENTIETH CENTURY

Lisa F. DeWitt

Illustrations by A. Mario Fantini

PRO LINGUA ASSOCIATES

Publisher

Published by Pro Lingua Associates
15 Elm Street
Brattleboro, Vermont 05301 USA

(802) 257-7779
SAN 216-0579

*At
Pro Lingua,
our objective is to foster
an approach to learning and teaching
that we call* Interplay, *the interaction of language
learners and teachers with their materials,
with the language and the culture, and
with each other in active, creative,
and productive
play.*

ISBN 0-86647-077-8

Cue Cards: Famous Women of the Twentieth Century was
set in Andover type with Colonial heads by Stevens Graphics
in Brattleboro, Vermont, and printed and bound by Braun-
Brumfield in Ann Arbor, Michigan.

Designed by Arthur A. Burrows.

Printed in the United States of America

Acknowledgements

I would like to acknowledge the assistance and inspiration I got from Patricia, Bertina, and Camilla Daniél, who helped me in the very difficult task of selecting only 40 famous women. Thanks also to my editor, Ray Clark, my typist, Vera Mitchell, and my Mother. I'd like to dedicate my efforts to my daughter, Allegra Maria Torres.

L.F.D.

FAMOUS WOMEN
OF THE TWENTIETH CENTURY

1. ## Dr. Elizabeth Blackwell
   1821–1910   England   Educator; Medical Doctor

2. ## Marie Curie
   1867–1934   Poland   Scientist

3. ## Madame C. J. Walker
   1867–1919   U.S.A.   Businesswoman

4. ## Maria Montessori
   1870–1952   Italy   Medical Doctor; Educator

5. ## Helena Rubenstein
   1870–1965   Poland   Cosmetician; Businesswoman

6. ## Elizabeth Arden
   1878–1966   Canada   Cosmetician; Businesswoman

7. ## Margaret Sanger
   1879–1966   U.S.A.   Nurse; Birth Control Advocate

8. ## Helen Keller
   1880–1968   U.S.A.   Writer; Advocate for the Blind

9. ## Anna Pavlova
   1882–1931   Russia   Ballerina

10. ## Coco Chanel
    1883–1971   France   Fashion Designer; Businesswoman

11. ## Eleanor Roosevelt
    1884–1962   U.S.A.   Human Service

12. ## Isak Dinesen
    1885–1962   Denmark   Writer

27. "Babe" Didrickson Zaharias
   1914–1956   U.S.A.   Athlete

28. Indira Gandhi
   1917–1984   India   Political Leader

29. Eva Perón
   1919–1952   Argentina   Political Leader

30. Nadine Gordimer
   1923–   South Africa   Writer

31. Shirley Chisholm
   1924–   U.S.A.   Political Leader; Educator

32. Margaret Thatcher
   1925–   England   Political Leader

33. Elisabeth Kübler-Ross
   1926–   Switzerland   Psychiatrist

34. Barbara Walters
   1931–   U.S.A.   TV Journalist

35. Dian Fossey
   1932–1985   U.S.A.   Conservationist

36. Gloria Steinem
   1934–   U.S.A.   Writer; Feminist

37. Alice Walker
   1944–   U.S.A.   Writer

38. Aung San Suu Kyi
   1945–   Myanmar   Political Leader

39. Joan Benoit Samuelson
   1957–   U.S.A.   Athlete

40. Rigoberta Menchú
   1959–   Guatemala   Human Rights Activist

CONTENTS

INTRODUCTION

This collection of Cue Cards — the stories or bio-sketches of 40 women who shaped the 20th century — really needs no introduction. Each woman's life story speaks for itself.

In the language classroom, as students tell and listen to these stories, they will not only practice using the language in connected discourse, they will also share in the triumphs and tragedies of these fascinating people.

There are 40 cards in this collection. They are basically similar, because each one is a biographical sketch. Although certain words, phrases, and grammatical structures recur throughout the collection, each card is distinct. The card format also offers a great deal of flexibility in the way it is used in the classroom. We have provided some ideas in the next few paragraphs, but we hope you will appreciate and take advantage of the possibilities available to you because of the openness of the format.

Students at all levels can use these cards. Beginners may be able to use only the initial introductory information easily, but we have made a conscious effort to use prose that is direct and transparent, and so even beginners can skim the cards, finding key words, phrases, and dates for contructing a simple re-telling of the woman's life.

Students at the intermediate and advanced levels can obviously make greater use of these cards. The material is not designed to teach new words or grammatical structures, although language acquisition is bound to occur as the students use the cards. The primary purpose is to stimulate speaking practice, both conversational back-and-forth and connected narrative discourse, as one student relates the story to another from beginning to end. It should be obvious that listening and, to a lesser extent, reading will also be practiced.

How to Use These Cue Cards

1. The Basic Technique

It is quite simple. Give each student a card. Have students read through the cards silently as you circulate to help with the comprehension. When all have finished reading, pair the students. The two students then take turns telling each other about the life story on the card. You should encourage them to only glance at the card for facts and continuity. They should *tell, not read*. When they have finished, they split up and find somebody else to exchange stories with. This continues until the activity begins to wear thin.

2. Conversation Practice

Give each student a card, allowing a few minutes to study the card for comprehension. Help students with any questions they might have, then pair them and have them take the part of the person on their cards and carry out a question/ answer "getting to know you" conversation. They can then split up and find new partners.

3. Introduction

Pair two students and have them carry out a conversation practice as described above. Then, one by one, the pairs introduce their new "friends" to others in the class.

4. Story-A-Day

Each day one student tells a story to the class.

5. Dictation

Dictate a story to the class. This can become very useful if done several times. Students can also give the dictation.

6. Interview

One student can be "Barbara Walters" and interview another student-as-famous-person, as the rest of the class is the studio audience. "Barbara" can ask the audience for questions.

7. Summit Meeting

Choose a group of women whose active lives overlap. Each student takes a card, studies it, and then role plays that woman at an "international women's congress." Ask the students to see if they can make connections, for example, Rubinstein-Arden, Roosevelt-Anderson. You can also give them an issue to share opinions on, such as, "What is the greatest problem facing women today?"

8. Listen and Take Notes

Give a mini-lecture on one of the women. Use the card for notes, but don't read it; deliver it like a lecture. Have the students take notes and then give them a short quiz to check the accuracy of their notes.

9. Press Conference

One student poses as one of the famous women. The others throw questions at her. Encourage the askers to ask questions that solicit opinion, for example, "What do you think about abortion?"

10. Research

Ask the students to choose a woman and find out more about her. Results can be reported orally or as a paper.

We are sure many of you will find some interesting ways to use these cards, and we would like to hear about them.

We hope you enjoy this collection.

R.C.C.

RELATED PRO LINGUA MATERIALS

Games and Activities

Cue Cards: Nations of the World by Raymond C. Clark and Anna Mussman. A set of 42 *Cue Cards* with detailed information about the most populous nations of the world.

Index Card Games for ESL, edited by Raymond C. Clark. Six game techniques using index cards with sample games at three levels, easy to difficult. Also available for French and Spanish.

More Index Card Games and Activities for English. Nine more game techniques including *Cue Cards* and *Story Cards*. There are sample games at three levels of difficulty.

Operations in English by Gayle Nelson and Thomas Winters. 55 operations, games, and communicative activities effective with beginning to intermediate students. Useful with a wide variety of approaches from audio-lingual to the Silent Way, from Total Physical Response to the Natural Approach.

Story Cards: The Tales of Nasreddin Hodja by Raymond C. Clark. 40 stories for building story-telling and other communicative skills.

Conversation Inspirations by Nancy Zellman. Over 1200 topics to talk about, using six techniques for effective conversation classes.

Families: 10 Card Games for Language Learners by Marjorie S. Fuchs, Jane Critchley, and Thomas Pyle. 40 brightly colored playing cards with eight vocabulary items to ask questions about: clothing, shoes, hats, numbers/money, things carried, time, transportation, colors, and facial expressions.

Discovery Trail: *Basic ESL Kit* by Mark Feder. A board game with question cards on English grammar (three levels), prepositions, and proverbs. Available separately: 2-word verbs, American idioms, geography and history (world facts and U.S. facts), and U.S. citizenship.

For further information or to order, please write to:
Pro Lingua Associates, 15 Elm St., Brattleboro, Vermont 05301 *or call us at* **800-366-4775.**
We accept **VISA** *and* **MasterCard** *orders by phone.*

Cue Cards

FAMOUS WOMEN
OF THE
TWENTIETH CENTURY

HOW TO PREPARE YOUR CUE CARDS

This set of Cue Cards has been bound as a book for ease of handling and to save you money. To prepare the cards for use, follow these easy steps.

1. Tear the cards out of the book at the perforation. This will leave a slightly rough edge which you may wish to trim.

2. These cards should be durable enough for several years of use, but they will last longer if laminated.

3. Keep the introductory explanation and teaching ideas in a file for future use.

Dr. Elizabeth Blackwell

"The new hope for the world that I see dawning with the advent of womanhood into the realm of independent thought and equal justice makes me very happy." (written in 1887)

Born: February 3, 1821, in Bristol, England.

Died: May 31, 1910.

Education: Geneva Medical School, New York; graduated in 1849.

Occupation: Educator and Physician.

1. Breaking New Ground

In 1849, Dr. Elizabeth Blackwell was the first woman to graduate in medicine. By special permission she had attended Geneva College (now Hobart College) in New York State. She was also the first woman in the United States to qualify as a doctor. By 1889 there were three thousand women doctors in the United States; by 1900 seven thousand. However, in 1991 only 15.8% of all doctors in the United States were women.

2. Breaking Traditions

When Elizabeth was a child she moved with her family to New York City, where she attended school. Her father was unlike most men of his time as he believed in equal education for both girls and boys. He encouraged his daughters to develop their minds.

The Blackwell home was opened to many influential people, including nurse Florence Nightingale. The Blackwell family belonged to the Anti-Slavery Society and also worked for the suffrage movement — women's right to vote. There is no doubt that Elizabeth was, therefore, well prepared to break the tradition of "no women doctors."

3. The First Women's Hospital

Elizabeth had been practicing medicine in New York City when she was joined by her younger sister, Emily, also a doctor. After fifteen years of careful planning and raising thirty thousand dollars, the two Blackwell doctors opened the New York Infirmary for Indigent Women and Children, on May 12, 1857. Elizabeth chose this date because it was the birthday of Florence Nightingale, who had been such an inspiration for her.

The hospital was the first with an all-woman staff. It later expanded to include a women's medical college. It was the first to train nurses; to train a black woman doctor, Rebecca Cole; to require a four-year course of study; to have a cancer prevention and treatment clinic. It also set the standards for hospital hygiene. It still stands today on Stuyvesant Square in New York City.

4. The Standard of Excellence

Dr. Elizabeth Blackwell is honored every year at Hobart and William Smith Colleges, when an award is given in her name to a woman who exemplifies "unselfish devotion, sense of dedication, and reverence for life." Dr. Blackwell had not only opened the door for women to become doctors but had also set the standards of excellence for medical education and practice.

Famous Women
of the Twentieth Century
Lisa F. DeWitt

Cue Cards

PRO LINGUA ● ASSOCIATES

Famous Women
of the Twentieth Century
Lisa F. DeWitt

Marie Curie

"I am among those who think science has great beauty. A scientist in his laboratory is not only a technician; he is also a child placed before natural phenomena which impress him like a fairy tale."

Born: November 7, 1867, in Warsaw, Poland.

Died: July 4, 1934.

Education: 1894 graduate — Sorbonne, Paris, France; degrees in physical science and mathematics.

Occupation: Inventor, scientist, professor.

Honors: Nobel Prize in Physics — 1903. Nobel Prize in Chemistry — 1911. The first person ever to win two Nobel prizes.

1. Manya-Marie

Marie Curie, nee Manya Sklodovska, is generally thought of as the greatest woman scientist of all time. She was a brilliant student, excelling in science, math, and languages. Both she and her older sister, Bronya, wanted to work in the field of science. Bronya wanted to be a medical doctor, and so for four years Manya worked as a governess to help put Bronya through medical school in Paris. Then after Bronya became a doctor, she helped her younger sister, Manya, become the first woman to be admitted to the Sorbonne in Paris, in 1891. Shortly after her arrival, she changed her name from Manya to Marie, adopting the French version of her name. She graduated in 1894. While at school she met Pierre Curie, and they later married, in 1895.

2. The Curies

Pierre and Marie worked together and set up a small laboratory at their home in an old shed. In 1897 their first daughter, Irène, was born. Marie continued her work in studying uranium and the rays it gave out. Together Maria and Pierre discovered radium and polonium, and worked to further isolate and study the properties of these two elements. Radium proved to be one of the world's great discoveries and medical benefits. In 1903 Marie and Pierre were awarded the Nobel Prize in Physics. Then in 1906 a tragedy: Pierre was killed as he stepped out from his cab and was crushed by a heavy horse-drawn wagon. But Marie continued working and was asked by the Sorbonne to take Pierre's place at the University. She became the first woman professor at the Sorbonne and the first at any French university.

3. Ambassador for Science

In 1910, Marie published "Treatise on Radioactivity," which was a complete account of her discoveries about radioactivity. She was awarded a second Nobel Prize, this time in Chemistry, and became the first person to receive the award twice.

The Sorbonne built for Marie, in honor of Pierre, a special institute for the study of radium. The Radium Institute was finished on July 13, 1914. Marie, however, delayed work at the institute to volunteer her services to helping wounded soldiers during World War I.

She later returned to the Radium Institute and established a course to instruct technicians in radiology. Her daughter, Irène, was working at the institute by this time.

In 1921 Marie visited the United States and then became an ambassador for science. She traveled to many different countries and universities, encouraging new scientific research.

4. The Curie Work Continues.

Marie's health had been seriously affected by the years of exposure to radium and X-rays. She had aplastic pernicious anemia, which affects the production of bone marrow. On July 4, 1934, Marie Curie died. One year later, her daughter and son-in-law, Irène and Frédéric Joliot-Curie, received a Nobel Prize in Chemistry for the development of radioactive isotopes.

Cue Cards

**Famous Women
of the Twentieth Century
Lisa F. DeWitt**

PRO LINGUA ⬤ ASSOCIATES

**Famous Women
of the Twentieth Century
Lisa F. DeWitt**

Madame C. J. Walker

"America doesn't respect anything but money. You can struggle along sending out teachers, cramming book learning into children that haven't got shoes. What our people need is a few millionaires."

Born: December 23, 1867, in Delta, Louisiana.

Died: April 25, 1919, in New York.

Education: Self-educated.

Occupation: Businesswoman.

Honors: Named to *Ebony* magazine's "Hall of Fame." First black woman millionaire in the United States.

1. The Early Years

Sarah Breedlove was born into hardship on a Louisiana farm. She was an orphaned child who married when she was only fourteen. She had one child, a daughter, A'lelia. When Sarah's husband died she was only twenty years old, and she moved with her young child to St. Louis, Missouri. For eighteen years she worked as a washerwoman, washing white people's clothing for only $1.50 a day.

2. Business Beginnings

Beginning with $5.00 as her total capital assets, Sarah began a small business in 1905. She made a treatment for straightening tightly curled hair. She also developed other hair care products and in 1906 she moved to Denver, Colorado. She later married Charles J. Walker, a news reporter, and was then always referred to as Madame C. J. Walker. Her business continued to grow, and she opened her corporate headquarters in Indianapolis, Indiana.

3. Growth

The Madame C. J. Walker Manufacturing Company employed over 3,000 people, mostly women. Madame Walker's salespeople sold her products door-to-door. They were trained to be well-groomed and thorough. The products were popular not only in the United States, but in Europe and the Caribbean. Madame Walker's business rivaled those of both Helena Rubenstein and Elizabeth Arden.

Madame Walker donated large sums of money to charity and organizations such as the N.A.A.C.P. (The National Association for the Advancement of Colored People).

4. Later Years

In 1914, she built a large home in New York City, and in 1917 she built another, a thirty-room estate on the Hudson River. After her death on April 25, 1919, her New York City home was opened to a number of black writers, artists, and musicians. Her daughter inherited her mother's business and the Walker Manufacturing Company still produces Madame Walker's original formulas today.

Famous Women
of the Twentieth Century
Lisa F. DeWitt

Cue Cards

PRO LINGUA ⬤ ASSOCIATES

Famous Women
of the Twentieth Century
Lisa F. DeWitt

Maria Montessori

"We teachers can only help the work going on, as servants wait upon a master."

Born: August 31, 1870, in Chiaraville, Italy.
Died: May 6, 1952.
Education: Medical degree — University of Rome — 1896.
Occupation: Doctor of Medicine, Educator, and Writer.

1. The "Montessori Miracle"

Maria Montessori grew up in Chiaraville, Italy. She excelled in mathematics and wanted to pursue a career in engineering. At the time, the only profession for women was teaching. When she entered the University of Rome she decided to study medicine. She studied pediatrics in the last two years of medical school and became the first woman to graduate from the University's School of Medicine, in 1896.

She returned to the University to do research work at the psychiatric clinic. As part of her job, she visited insane asylums to choose patients for treatment at the clinic. Her special interest was in children. In 1898 she was appointed director of the Orthophrenic Institute in Rome, an institution devoted to the care and education of retarded children.

She learned from her work with retarded children that they were capable of learning and functioning productively and even creatively. They passed state examinations in reading and writing, achieving scores that were higher than those of "normal" children.

2. The Development of The Montessori Method

Dr. Montessori put her theories, methods, and materials into practice in 1907 when she began working in the slum section of Rome —San Lorenzo. She worked in the Casa dei Bambini children's house, which took in children between the ages of three and seven while their parents were working. She found that children thrived on the activity involved with learning and that the best form of punishment was inactivity.

The Montessori Method was born and Dr. Maria Montessori soon became the world's foremost female educator and advocate of pre-school education. Her first book was published in 1909 and was considered by educators to be a very important work. It was later translated into most of the major languages of the world; the English translation is *The Montessori Method*.

3. Definition of the Method

The method is based on giving children freedom in a specially prepared environment, under the guidance of a trained teacher. It strives to develop self-discipline and self-confidence in children by allowing them to follow their own interests when they are ready to learn to find out things for themselves. They usually read and write by the age of five or six.

The Montessori materials are basically divided into four categories: the daily-living exercises involving the physical care of person and environment; the sensorial, the academic, and the cultural and artistic materials.

4. Influence of the Method

From 1909 until her death, Dr. Montessori devoted her life to spreading the word of the Montessori method, and she traveled extensively giving lectures and setting up teacher-training courses around the world.

Today, her method is part of every college teacher-training course, and her philosophy and materials are used in public schools, special education, and pre-schools, as well as private Montessori schools, which can be found in virtually every country.

Cue Cards

**Famous Women
of the Twentieth Century
Lisa F. DeWitt**

PRO LINGUA ⬤ ASSOCIATES

**Famous Women
of the Twentieth Century
Lisa F. DeWitt**

Helena Rubinstein

"I have always felt that a woman has the right to treat the subject of her age with ambiguity until, perhaps, she passes into the realm of over ninety."

Born: December 25, 1870 (approximately), in Cracow, Poland.

Died: April 1, 1965.

Education: Attended the University of Cracow; studied medicine in Switzerland.

Occupation: Entrepreneur.

1. The Salons

In 1902 Helena Rubinstein immigrated alone to Australia. She took with her twelve pots of her mother's face cream developed by a chemist in Poland. It wasn't long before she opened a shop in Melbourne, instructing women on the art of proper skin care and selling her "crème valaz," a cream for sunburned Australian complexions. Her shop was a success, and Helena worked eighteen hours a day, something she did throughout her life. Her sister later joined her in Australia and ran the business there while Helena set off to London to begin her international organization and open another salon.

In 1915 Helena and her husband, Edward Titus, an American newspaperman, and their two sons left for America. Rubinstein's Maison de Beauté in Manhattan was soon opened, and by 1917 there were salons in San Francisco, Boston, and Philadelphia as well.

2. Rivalry

Near Rubinstein's Maison de Beauté was Elizabeth Arden's salon on Fifth Avenue. They were not friendly rivals. They were very competitive. When Arden hired eleven of Rubinstein's best employees, Rubinstein hired Arden's ex-husband. After Rubinstein married a Russian prince in 1938, Arden married a prince in 1942. Arden did outlive Rubinstein, however, but only by eighteen months.

3. That's Business.

Although only four feet ten inches tall, Helena Rubinstein was a formidable business force. To slow her life down, she sold her American business for $3 million, and then a year later, in 1929, after the great stock market crash, she bought it back for $1.5 million. Helena was known for her bold business deals. For example, when she was told that she couldn't rent the penthouse apartment in a chic Park Avenue complex, because Jews were not allowed, she bought the entire building.

4. No Retirement

Helena Rubinstein never retired and even conducted business from her bed when she was in her nineties. She remained in charge and hired many family members to carry on her business.

Her estate was valued at more than $130 million at the time of her death. The company still exists today.

Cue Cards

**Famous Women
of the Twentieth Century
Lisa F. DeWitt**

PRO LINGUA ● ASSOCIATES

**Famous Women
of the Twentieth Century
Lisa F. DeWitt**

Copyright © 1993 by Pro Lingua Associates, Address: 15 Elm Street, Brattleboro, Vermont 05301 U.S.A. Telephone: 800-366-4775.

Elizabeth Arden

"Dear, never forget one little point: It's my business. You just work here."

Born: December 31, 1878 (approximately), in the village of Woodbridge near Toronto, Canada.

Died: October 18, 1966.

Education: Attended high school.

Occupation: Entrepreneur.

1. What's in a name?

Florence Nightingale Graham was thirty years old when she finally found her life's work. Before this she worked at a variety of jobs, including dental assistant, cashier, and stenographer. When she moved to New York City she worked for the English cosmetic firm Eleanor Adair. While there, she was trained as a facial masseuse. Florence was a good advertisement for the business because of her own naturally beautiful complexion.

She soon opened a salon with a business partner, Elizabeth Hubbard, on Fifth Avenue. Florence, however, wanted to be the sole owner of her own business; something that she managed to achieve and maintain throughout her life. So the partnership soon ended.

Florence removed Hubbard's last name from the salon's nameplate and added Arden. She started her new life with her new name, Elizabeth Arden, although she never legally changed it.

2. Developments

In 1914 Elizabeth Arden began to travel to Europe, where she researched beauty techniques and products. In 1915 she expanded her New York salon and opened branches in Boston and Washington, D.C. Her salons were known for three things: Amoretta cleansing cream, Adrena skin toner, and facial massage.

She also helped formulate the first non-greasy skin cream. She introduced lipstick shades coordinated to skin tone and clothing and developed makeup foundations. By the 1920's, Arden had more than a hundred salon locations. The company took in about 60 million dollars in annual sales.

3. Kentucky Derby

Arden also loved horses and made a fortune in horse racing. In 1930 she bought a horse farm in Lexington, Kentucky, and her horses won many races. Then in 1947 her horse — Jet Pilot — won the Kentucky Derby, the most important horse race in the United States.

4. Archrival

Helena Rubinstein, whose business was on 49th Street near Arden's on Fifth Avenue, was an archrival. Arden had traveled the world visiting beauty salons but never once visited anyone at Rubinstein's.

When she hired away eleven of Rubinstein's best employees, Rubinstein hired Arden's ex-husband, who had remained Arden's employee after their divorce. The newspapers and magazines at the time loved to write about these two archrivals. Arden outlived Rubinstein, but by only eighteen months.

Famous Women of the Twentieth Century
Lisa F. DeWitt

Cue Cards

PRO LINGUA ● ASSOCIATES

Famous Women of the Twentieth Century
Lisa F. DeWitt

Margaret Sanger

"A woman must make herself the absolute mistress of her own body."

Born: September 14, 1879, in Corning, New York.

Died: September 6, 1966.

Education: Attended Claverack College in New York and the White Plains Hospital School of Nursing.

Occupation: Nurse and birth control advocate.

1. First Woman Birth Control Advocate

Margaret Sanger was the first woman to advocate sex education and birth control for women. She grew up as one of eleven children. Her mother, who worked hard but had little money to care for them, died at forty-nine. That may have caused Margaret to become the passionate spokeswoman for a woman's right to have control of her own body.

After moving to New York City and working as a nurse, she began to establish herself as a writer and educator on sexual reform and birth control.

2. First Birth Control Clinic

Margaret traveled to Europe to research the subject of female birth control. While she was in Europe she observed many contraceptive clinics in the Netherlands. In 1914 she published *The Woman Rebel*, and in 1916, she opened the first U.S. birth control clinic, in Brooklyn, New York. It was soon closed down and Margaret was jailed. She used the trial as an opportunity to publicize the need for giving advice about contraception to women.

3. Planned Parenthood and the Pill

By November 2, 1921, there was enough public support and money to establish the American Birth Control League. Then in 1923, Margaret Sanger opened the first birth control clinic and research bureau staffed by physicians. She helped to form the International Planned Parenthood Federation and supported the development of the birth control pill for women.

4. Followers of Margaret Sanger

The Pulitzer Prize-winning journalist Susan Faludi, in her book *Backlash: The Undeclared War Against American Women*, writes, ". . . the birth control movement that Margaret Sanger launched enjoyed far broader appeal than any other plank of the women's rights campaign, cutting across class and race lines. We must all be followers of Margaret Sanger."

Famous Women
of the Twentieth Century
Lisa F. DeWitt

Cue Cards

PRO LINGUA  ASSOCIATES

Famous Women
of the Twentieth Century
Lisa F. DeWitt

Helen Keller

"You came and opened life's shut portals and let in joy, hope, knowledge, and friendship . . . God bless you my teacher from everlasting to everlasting."

Born: June 17, 1880, in Tuscumbia, Alabama.

Died: June 1, 1968.

Education: tutored by Anne Sullivan Macy; Perkins School for the Blind, Watertown, Massachusetts; graduated cum laude, 1904, from Radcliffe College, Cambridge, Massachusetts.

Occupation: Writer, speaker, and advocate for the blind.

1. "Living in a No-World"

Helen Keller began life as a normal seeing, hearing child, but when she was nineteen months old she suddenly became ill with a high fever. The illness left her blind, deaf, and unable to speak. For seven years she lived in her own dark, silent world. Helen describes herself at that time as "a phantom living in a no-world." Her mind, however, was clear and active. She would often have tantrums because she was unable to be understood or be part of life.

2. Teacher

On March 3, 1887, Helen Keller's world changed forever. Anne Sullivan, a twenty-year-old graduate from the Perkins School for the Blind, had arrived at the Keller home. Helen later wrote of that day as "my soul's birthday." It is impossible to speak of Helen Keller's life and accomplishments without understanding the importance of her teacher.

Anne Sullivan had been taken to a Massachusetts poorhouse as a half-blind ten-year-old. For three years she lived in horrible conditions. Then one day when inspectors came to inspect the poorhouse, Anne cried out that she wanted to go to school. One of the inspectors made the arrangements and Anne started studies at the Perkins School on October 3, 1880. She later had two operations that improved her eyesight. Her first job after Perkins was tutoring Helen Keller. This job she did for fifty years, until her death on October 20, 1936.

3. The Miracle Worker

Helen was a bright child and learned very quickly. With Anne, she first learned that everything had a name and that the manual alphabet was the key to everything she wanted to know. This early learning was written about in William Gibson's play *The Miracle Worker*, which was later made into an Academy Award-winning film. It was a miracle that Anne Sullivan had unlocked Helen's mind and given her the keys to a new world. Helen always lovingly called Anne "Teacher," and whatever she accomplished in her life Helen always credited to "Teacher."

4. Service

Helen made her living by inspiring others through her lectures and writing. She met U.S. Presidents; Winston Churchill asked to meet her; Prime Minister Nehru was enchanted by her. Among her friends were Alexander Graham Bell, Eleanor Roosevelt, and Mark Twain. She was invited to feel a dance rehearsal with Martha Graham. Philanthropist Andrew Carnegie gave her an annual pension so that she could continue her good works. Helen Keller lived a full and rewarding life, and she gave hope and inspiration to many.

Famous Women
of the Twentieth Century
Lisa F. DeWitt

Cue Cards

PRO LINGUA ⬤ ASSOCIATES

Famous Women
of the Twentieth Century
Lisa F. DeWitt

Anna Pavlova

"No one can arrive from being talented alone. God gives talent, work transforms talent into genius."

Born: January 31, 1882, in St. Petersburg, Russia.

Died: January 23, 1931.

Education: Imperial Ballet School in St. Petersburg.

Occupation: Prima ballerina.

1. From Peasant to Princess to Prima

Anna Pavlova was born of peasant parents and was a sickly, premature infant. As a frail child she almost died twice from scarlet fever and diphtheria. When she was about eight years old, she saw the ballet *The Sleeping Beauty*, and from that moment on she was determined to be a ballerina.

When she was ten, she persuaded the examiners at the Imperial Ballet School in St. Petersburg to admit her as a student. She made her debut in 1899 at age seventeen dancing the principal character, Princess Aurora, in *The Sleeping Beauty*. Her extraordinary talents were rewarded in 1906, when she received the highest title of prima ballerina.

2. The Tours

From 1907 until 1908 she toured with the Russian Imperial Ballet, dancing in various cities in northern Europe. She also performed with the Diaghilev Ballet Russes in Paris and London in 1909 and 1911. She appeared at the Metropolitan Opera House in New York in 1910. Then in 1912, she resigned from the Imperial Ballet to make a worldwide tour with her own company. She danced in major cities and in small villages and towns throughout the world.

She learned the dances of many of the countries she visited and used them in her repertory. She had introduced ballet to millions who otherwise would probably never have known its beauty.

3. *The Dying Swan*

The Dying Swan is a four-minute solo work that the famous Russian choreographer, Michel Fokine, wrote for Anna Pavlova. It was to become her most famous role, and it is said that she could reduce grown men and women to tears when she danced it.

In January, 1931, Anna contracted pneumonia. She was scheduled to perform *The Dying Swan* at the Hague Theatre in the Netherlands on January 23. As she lay dying, she whispered, "Prepare my Swan costume." A short time later she died. The following night during the scheduled time in the program for her performance in *The Dying Swan*, the curtain went up on an empty stage. The audience stood in tribute to one of the greatest ballet dancers of the 20th century.

Famous Women
of the Twentieth Century
Lisa F. DeWitt

Cue Cards

PRO LINGUA  ASSOCIATES

Famous Women
of the Twentieth Century
Lisa F. DeWitt

Coco Chanel

"There are too many men in this business and they don't know how to make clothes for women."

Born: August 19, 1883, outside of Paris, France.

Died: January 10, 1971.

Education: No formal education.

Occupation: Fashion designer.

1. A Born Designer

Gabrielle Bonheur Chanel was born outside of Paris, France, and because she was orphaned at the age of six, she was brought up by her two aunts in the rural province of Auvergne. Her aunts tried to teach her to sew, something they thought girls should know how to do. Gabrielle never learned how to sew well, but she did design hats and clothes. She began by cutting her aunts' drapes and making clothes for her doll. When she was seventeen she joined her sister in Deauville and opened her own hat shop.

2. Coco

Gabrielle loved to go horseback riding early in the morning when the cocks were crowing. She was thereafter nicknamed Miss Cocorico (French for the cock's "cock-a-doodle-do"), which was later shortened to Coco — "little pet."

Her hat business was doing well, and in 1914 she added her own line of clothes. From then on her designs were in demand, and she was always known as "Coco."

3. Success

At the height of her career, she ran four separate businesses: textile, costume, jewelry design, and perfume. The headquarters of the businesses was at 31 rue Cambon in Paris.

She designed her first perfume in 1922 and bottled it in simple bottles, calling it Chanel No. 5, because five was her lucky number. It is still one of the most famous, best-selling perfumes in the world.

It was during the 20's that Coco became the fashion queen of Paris, with a million-dollar business.

4. Out of Retirement

At the beginning of World War II she closed all except her perfume business. After fifteen years, however, she returned because she was upset that Paris fashion had been taken over by men, who, in her opinion, didn't know how to design clothes for women.

In 1954, Coco again showed her line of clothes, and the tweed Chanel suit became famous; it is still popular today.

5. Fashion for the 20th Century

She wanted women to look pretty and youthful and to be comfortable in their clothes. This is why her fashion innovations have remained a part of the basic wardrobes of women for generations. By the time of her death, her fashion empire was earning over $160 million a year. Coco Chanel remains one of the most influential designers in the history of fashion design.

Famous Women
of the Twentieth Century
Lisa F. DeWitt

Cue Cards

PRO LINGUA ● ASSOCIATES

Famous Women
of the Twentieth Century
Lisa F. DeWitt

Eleanor Roosevelt

"When you cease to make a contribution you begin to die."

Born: October 11, 1884, in New York City, New York.

Died: November 7, 1962.

Education: Allenswood School for Girls outside of London, England.

Occupation: Social worker, teacher, First Lady, columnist, U.S. delegate to the United Nations.

1. The Early Years

Eleanor Roosevelt was raised in a wealthy home, but her childhood was without warmth and affection. She and her brother, Hall, were orphaned when she was ten, and until the age of fifteen she lived with her maternal grandmother. She was a shy and unhappy child who felt that she was unattractive.

Then she attended Allenswood, a private girls' school outside of London, from 1899 to 1902. At Allenswood, she found friendship and the loving guidance of the school's headmistress, Marie Souvestre. These three years changed Eleanor's life, and she excelled in her studies and was also very well liked. When she returned to the United States she devoted herself to settlement work, helping immigrants adjust to living in the United States. For the rest of her life Eleanor worked to help those in need.

2. Politics

On March 17, 1905, Eleanor married her distant cousin, Franklin Roosevelt. Between 1906 and 1916, she had six children, one of whom died in infancy. She was a housewife and homemaker, and when her husband became involved in politics she was his strongest supporter.

In 1921, when her husband contracted polio and lost the use of his legs, Eleanor was indispensable to her husband's position as Democratic Party Leader in New York. In 1928 Franklin became Governor of New York and Eleanor became a strong voice for minority groups and women. In 1932, when her husband became President, she greatly influenced the formation of many social programs.

During her years as First Lady, from 1932 to 1945, she was an eloquent advocate of civil rights. When a women's group prohibited the black opera singer, Marian Anderson, from performing at Constitution Hall in Washington, D.C., Eleanor resigned from the group and arranged for the concert to be held at the Lincoln Memorial, where Anderson sang for a crowd of seventy-five thousand people.

3. The Later Years

After her husband's death in 1945, Eleanor was appointed a delegate to the United Nations' Charter Commission. Later she became its chairman.

In 1953 she left the United Nations and worked for a nongovernmental organization, the American Association for the United Nations. She traveled to Hong Kong, Turkey, Greece, and Yugoslavia, and in 1957 she met with Premier Khrushchev in the USSR.

President Kennedy appointed her to the United Nations delegation in 1961, and she served in this position until her death.

Famous Women of the Twentieth Century
Lisa F. DeWitt

Cue Cards
PRO LINGUA ● ASSOCIATES

Famous Women of the Twentieth Century
Lisa F. DeWitt

Isak Dinesen

"As for me I have one ambition only: to invent stories, very beautiful stories."

Born: April 17, 1885, in Rungstedlund, Denmark.

Died: September 7, 1962.

Education: Attended the Royal Academy of Fine Art in Copenhagen, Denmark.

Occupation: Writer.

1. Karen, Baroness, and Isak Dinesen

Baroness Karen Blixen was born in 1885 in Rungstedlund, Denmark, and christened Karen Christentze Dinesen. She was forty-nine when she published her first book, *Seven Gothic Tales*, in 1934. She chose to write under the pseudonym Isak Dinesen, not to hide her feminine identity but to give herself freedom as a writer. She chose Dinesen because it was her father's family name and defines her roots and Isak, which is Hebrew for "laughter." And like the biblical Isaac, who was born when his mother Sarah was very old, Isak Dinesen as a creative person was born late.

2. *Out of Africa*

She would write in English first and then in Danish even though Danish was her native language. In 1914, she married Baron Blixen and moved with him to British East Africa. Her best-known book, *Out of Africa*, is about her life there: work on a coffee plantation, a love affair and the death of her lover, her husband's syphilis, their divorce in 1921, her management of the plantation, and its eventual failure. There is a blending of romance and realism, and she is a supreme story-teller.

It was her life's ambition to tell beautiful stories, and it was through her stories that she dealt with the pain and sorrow in her own life. She writes, "All sorrows can be borne if you put them into a story, or tell a story about them."

3. Back to Denmark

Baroness Karen Blixen had to leave Africa in 1931, because of the failure of her coffee plantation. She always longed to return to Africa, but twice her plans to return had to be cancelled because of ill health.

From 1934 to 1962 she wrote continuously and even after her death on April 7, 1962, her works were being published. In the 1940's she began to be recognized as a major author in her own country. In 1954, when Ernest Hemingway received the Nobel Prize for Literature, he said that she was really more deserving of the honor. Her work has had a powerful influence on the younger generation of Scandinavian writers today.

In 1985, *Out of Africa* was made into an award-winning movie, and her beautiful story was seen by millions.

Famous Women
of the Twentieth Century
Lisa F. DeWitt

Cue Cards

PRO LINGUA  ASSOCIATES

Famous Women
of the Twentieth Century
Lisa F. DeWitt

Georgia O'Keeffe

"Making an object look like what you see is not as important as making the whole square you paint on feel like what you feel about the object."

Born: November 15, 1887, in Sun Prairie, Wisconsin.

Died: March 6, 1986.

Education: Graduated in 1904 from Chatham Episcopal Institute in Williamsburg, Virginia; attended the Art Institute of Chicago, Columbia University, and the University of Virginia.

Occupation: Artist.

Honors: Creative Arts Award from Brandeis University — 1963. Gold Medal from National Institute of Arts and Letters — 1970. Medal of Freedom — given to her by President Carter — 1977.

1. Self-Expression

Georgia O'Keeffe has been called a "national treasure" and the most important woman artist in America. She is best known for her abstract paintings of flowers and desert landscapes of the Southwest, including cows' skulls, bare bones, the sky, clouds, and horizon lines. Her paintings are close-up studies that reduce the subjects to simplicity. It was always important to Georgia to express how she felt about the object she was painting, and it was only through her paintings that she felt free to express herself. "I found I could say things with color and shapes that I couldn't say in any other way — things I had no words for."

2. Becoming Known

In 1916, while Georgia was teaching art at a women's college in South Carolina, she sent her friend Anita Pollitzer some of her drawings, saying that she didn't want anyone else to see them. However, Anita was so excited about them that she showed them to Alfred Stieglitz, who had a Fifth Avenue art gallery — 291 — in New York City. Georgia later learned that Alfred had exhibited her drawings at 291. When she returned to New York she argued with Alfred about what he had done, but later she saw the benefits of exhibiting her drawings. She realized that Alfred had truly been touched by them. Alfred and Georgia later married. She continued to paint and exhibit and developed her unique style.

3. New Inspirations

In 1929 Georgia went to visit friends at Taos, an artists' community in northern New Mexico. She spent the summer there painting in an adobe art studio near a stream and became enthralled with the landscape. She knew that this was the place of her new inspirations, and she returned every summer. After Alfred's death in 1946 she moved to Abiguiu, near Santa Fe, and lived there for the remaining years of her life. She continued to paint, sculpt and travel, but she always came home to the mysterious desert landscape that fascinated her. She was ninety-eight years old when she died in Santa Fe.

Famous Women
of the Twentieth Century
Lisa F. DeWitt

Cue Cards

PRO LINGUA ● ASSOCIATES

Famous Women
of the Twentieth Century
Lisa F. DeWitt

Agatha Christie

"One of the pleasures of writing detective stories is that there are so many types to choose from: the light-hearted thriller . . . ; the intricate detective story with an involved plot . . . ; and then what I can only describe as the detective story that has a kind of passion behind it — that passion being to help save innocence. Because it is innocence that matters, not guilt."

Born: September 15, 1890, in Torquay, England.

Died: January 12, 1976.

Education: No formal education —home-tutored.

Occupation: Mystery writer.

Publications: Sixty-six crime novels, fifteen plays, two autobiographical works, two volumes of poems, one hundred fifty-seven short stories, and six novels under the pseudonym Mary Westmacott.

1. Childhood

Agatha Christie, born Agatha Mary Clarissa Miller, grew up in the seaside town of Torquay, England. Recalling her childhood, she writes: "One of the luckiest things that can happen to you in life is, I think, to have a happy childhood. I had a very happy childhood."

As a young child she showed a particular fascination for make-believe and story-telling. She loved books and taught herself to read before the age of five. She never attended school, but was home-tutored in writing and mathematics by her father and by a governess who taught her dressmaking and French. Agatha also traveled to other countries with her mother.

2. Mysterious Agatha

In 1909, she began her writing career at eighteen, when she wrote her first short story. Then in 1920 her first book was published in America, *The Mysterious Affair at Styles*. She then married Archibald Christie, had one child, Rosalind, and wrote four more novels. By 1926 she had become popular, but when *The Murder of Roger Ackroyd* was published in Britain, she became famous. Literary critics say that Agatha Christie's best work began with this book in 1926 and continued until the 1950s.

After its publication Agatha suddenly disappeared and became the object of a nationwide search. She was found ten days later, registered under the last name of her husband's mistress, at a hotel. She never explained her actions and soon after divorced her husband.

3. Hercule Poirot and Miss Marple

She continued to write a book every year. In 1930, she married archeologist Max Mallowan. Their years together were happy. "It's wonderful to be married to an archeologist —the older you get the more interested he is in you."

The two most popular detectives in her novels were Miss Marple, a spinster lady whom nobody notices but who sees everything, and Hercule Poirot, a retired Belgian detective, who is pretentious and meticulous.

In the 1940s she wrote their last cases, but requested that they not be published until after her death. Agatha Christie died on January 12, 1976, and both of her farewell books remained on the New York *Times* Bestseller List for many weeks.

4. "Queen of Crime"

By 1980 her books had sold over four hundred million copies, and had been translated into one hundred and three languages. She had become the most widely read British author in the world and the fifth best-selling author of all time. She was the "Queen of Crime."

Famous Women
of the Twentieth Century
Lisa F. DeWitt

Cue Cards

PRO LINGUA ● ASSOCIATES

Famous Women
of the Twentieth Century
Lisa F. DeWitt

Pearl S. Buck

"The minds of my own country and of China, my foster country, are alike in many ways, but above all, alike in our common·love of freedom."

Born: June 26, 1892, in Hillsboro, West Virginia.

Died: March 6, 1973.

Education: B.A., Randolph-Macon Women's College; M.A., Cornell University.

Occupation: Writer.

Honors: Pulitzer Prize for *The Good Earth* (1931); Nobel Prize in Literature (1938).

1. Two Worlds

Pearl S. Buck was only five months old when she sailed with her missionary parents to China. She was raised by a Chinese nurse, Wang Amah, whom she loved like a mother. In her autobiography, *My Several Worlds*, she writes: "When I was in the Chinese world, I was Chinese, I spoke Chinese, and behaved as a Chinese and ate as the Chinese did. I shared their thoughts and feelings. When I was in the American world, I shut the door between."

She began writing in 1922, and it was her many books, essays, articles, and short stories that opened the door between these two worlds. Throughout her writings the conflicts between East and West, old and new, are examined and explored.

2. *The Good Earth*

In 1931, her second novel, *The Good Earth*, was published. It was this novel that made Pearl S. Buck famous. It is a realistic story of a Chinese peasant family. The book was awarded the Pulitzer Prize in 1932; it was on the best seller list for months, sold over two million copies, was translated into over thirty languages, was adapted for a Broadway play, and was made into an award-winning Hollywood movie. In 1938, Pearl S. Buck became the first American woman to receive a Nobel Prize in Literature.

3. One Family

In her personal life she expressed her concerns for global understanding by creating an international family of ten children: one her natural daughter, and nine adopted children of different nationalities.

In 1949 she established Welcome House, an adoption agency for Asian-Americans.

Later, in 1964, the Pearl S. Buck Foundation was established to assist fatherless and often stateless, half-American children throughout Asia.

4. A Prolific Writer

Pearl S. Buck continued to write until her death. She wrote over 100 books about China, women's rights, work and marriage, racism, interracial marriage, the development of the atomic bomb, and her experiences as the mother of a retarded daughter. But she will always be remembered best for being China's most famous, unofficial, Western interpreter.

Famous Women
of the Twentieth Century
Lisa F. DeWitt

Cue Cards

PRO LINGUA ⬤ ASSOCIATES

Famous Women
of the Twentieth Century
Lisa F. DeWitt

Martha Graham

"Dance is the hidden language of the soul."

Born: May 11, 1894, in Allegheny, Pennsylvania.

Died: April 1, 1991.

Education: Cumnock School of Expression, Los Angeles; Denishawn Dance School, Los Angeles.

Occupation: Dancer, teacher, choreographer.

Honors: From 1932 to 1991 received over 37 different awards and honors from the U.S., France, Italy, Sweden, and Japan.

1. The Technique

Martha Graham is credited with single-handedly inventing a revolutionary new dance language. Her dance technique is called the Graham and is the basis for all modern dance that we see today. The technique, which is taught the world over, focuses on the center of the body — the solar-plexus — as being the source of energy and emotion.

2. The Career

Martha Graham moved from Pennsylvania to Santa Barbara, California, with her family in 1909. In 1911 her father took her to the Mason Opera House in Los Angeles to see an innovative dancer; her name was Ruth St. Denis. It was then that Martha knew she wanted to be a dancer and so, after high school, she enrolled in the Cumnock School of Expression in Los Angeles.

Then in 1916, after she graduated, she enrolled in the new School of Dancing and Related Arts, started by Ruth St. Denis in Los Angeles. In 1915 and again in 1916 Martha Graham saw the famous Russian ballerina, Anna Pavlova, dance at the Mason Opera House.

In 1920, Martha made her debut with the Denishawn dance company. She also taught dance at Denishawn until she left in 1923.

She moved to New York City and danced in the Greenwich Village Follies from 1923 until 1925. By 1926 she had launched her own career as a dancer and choreographer and by 1930 founded her own dance company.

3. The Choreography

In 1932, she was the first dancer to receive a Guggenheim Fellowship. She later began to put more of her energy into choreographing original works. Her choreographic career was one of the longest and most fertile of any artist's in history. Martha retired from dancing in 1969, but she choreographed until her death on April 1, 1991, producing more than 180 original works on universal themes of love, death, and the cyclical nature of life.

Famous Women
of the Twentieth Century
Lisa F. DeWitt

Cue Cards

PRO LINGUA ● ASSOCIATES

Famous Women
of the Twentieth Century
Lisa F. DeWitt

Amelia Earhart

"Courage is the price that life exacts for granting peace."

Born: July 24, 1897, in Atchison, Kansas.

Died: (disappeared) July 2, 1937, somewhere over the Pacific Ocean.

Education: Attended Columbia University and the University of Southern California.

Occupation: Nurse's aide, social worker, aviator, aviation editor.

Honors: The Distinguished Flying Cross, The Cross of the French Legion of Honor, National Geographic Society Gold Medal.

1. First Lady of the Air

From early childhood Amelia Earhart showed courage and spirit in everything she did. She became a symbol of courage and the American spirit during the 1930s and was known as "Lady Lindy, First Lady of the Air": "Lady Lindy" because of physical and personality traits that were similar to those of Charles A. Lindbergh, Jr., a famous aviator, and "First Lady of the Air" because of her many accomplishments as a woman aviator.

2. Varied Interests, Many Jobs

Amelia's adventurous spirit led her to follow her many interests and to have as many as 28 different jobs. She was a nurse's aide in a military hospital in Canada during World War I, a part-time English teacher/social worker to foreign-born people at Purdue University, in Indiana, and an aviation editor for *Cosmopolitan* magazine. In 1919, she was a student at Columbia University, but after one year she moved to California to join her family. She began taking flying lessons in California when she was twenty-three years old, and in 1923 she earned her pilot's license.

3. Aviation Accomplishments

In 1927, while Amelia was working in Boston, she was offered an opportunity to be the first woman to cross the Atlantic, not as the pilot, but as one of the crew members. The flight was arranged by publisher George Putnam, whom Amelia later married, in 1931. Then on May 21, 1932, Amelia became the first woman pilot to fly solo across the Atlantic. On August 24, 1932, she was the first woman pilot to complete a transcontinental flight, from New Jersey to California. On January 11, 1935, she completed the first solo flight from Hawaii to North America. She also set records in flying times.

4. The *Electra* and the Final Flight

Amelia's Lockheed plane, the *Electra*, was the newest type and design. It was given to her by Purdue University while she was a visiting faculty member there. In February 1937 Amelia said, "I think I have just one more long flight in my system." She wanted to fly around the world in the *Electra*. Amelia began her around-the-world flight on June 1, 1937, with one crew member, Fred Noonan. Then on July 2, 1937, while they were flying from New Guinea to Howland Island in the Pacific Ocean, radio contact with the *Electra* was lost. No trace of Amelia, Fred, or the *Electra* has ever been found.

**Famous Women
of the Twentieth Century
Lisa F. DeWitt**

Cue Cards

PRO LINGUA ⬤ ASSOCIATES

**Famous Women
of the Twentieth Century
Lisa F. DeWitt**

Golda Meir

"To be successful, a woman has to be much better at her job than a man."

Born: May 3, 1898, in Kiev, Ukraine.

Died: December 8, 1978.

Education: 1917 graduate — Milwaukee Normal School for Teachers.

Occupation: Various political offices in Israel and Prime Minister of Israel (1969-1974).

1. Making Speeches

Golda Mabovitz was born in Kiev, Ukraine in 1898. At the time, being a Jew there meant living a life of terror and uncertainty. The Czar's soldiers would ride through the Jewish communities destroying them. In 1906, Golda emigrated to Milwaukee, Wisconsin, with her family.

Golda learned English quickly and was an excellent student. She was also becoming politically aware and active even as a schoolgirl. Golda would stand on a box on a street corner and make speeches about what was happening to the Jews throughout Europe. Golda and others who believed that the Jews needed their own homeland were called Zionists.

2. The Kibbutz

Later, in 1917, Golda married Morris Meyerson, and in 1921 they left for Palestine. They joined a kibbutz, which is a small community of people working together and sharing everything they earn and own. She loved living on the kibbutz, but her husband did not enjoy the hard work and wanted to leave; and so, regretfully, Golda left with her husband to live and work in Tel Aviv and then Jerusalem. They had two children, but in 1945 Golda and Morris separated. Morris died in 1951.

3. Politics

While her children were still young, Golda became involved in politics. On May 14, 1948, she was among the signers of the Declaration of Independence of the State of Israel. She was the only woman member of the new government. She held several other positions before she was elected Israel's fourth Prime Minister at age 71. She served from 1969 until 1974.

4. Arab Territories

She resigned in April 1974 because her cabinet could not agree on what to do with the Arab territories. She was in favor of returning the Sinai to Egypt and the Golan Heights to Syria, and permitting the West Bank of Jordan to became an independent part of the Kingdom of Jordan. She wanted "secure, recognized and agreed boundaries," as part of a general peace settlement with the Arab nations.

5. The "Uncrowned Queen of Israel"

When she died, among the world leaders who attended her funeral was President Anwar Sadat of Egypt, which had been an enemy of Israel.

Tens of thousands of Israelis passed her simple coffin, which was draped in the Israeli flag, and nearly 100 national leaders attended her funeral. Golda Meir will be remembered as the "uncrowned Queen of Israel."

**Famous Women
of the Twentieth Century
Lisa F. DeWitt**

Cue Cards

PRO LINGUA ⬤ ASSOCIATES

**Famous Women
of the Twentieth Century
Lisa F. DeWitt**

Margaret Mead

"We need every human gift and cannot afford to neglect any gift because of artificial barriers of sex or race or class or national origin."

Born: December 16, 1901, in Philadelphia, Pennsylvania.

Died: November 15, 1978.

Education: B.A., Barnard College, New York, 1923. M.A., Psychology, Columbia University, New York, 1924. Ph.D., Anthropology, Columbia University, New York, 1929.

Occupation: Anthropologist, writer, and museum curator.

1. Science and Humanity

Margaret's grandmother, a child psychologist, taught Margaret at the age of eight how to take notes on people's behavior. This was a skill that Margaret Mead later excelled in, and in her career as a social and cultural anthropologist, she wrote hundreds of articles and twenty-three books.

Her first book, *Coming of Age in Samoa*, was based on her research on the small island of Tau in Samoa. It was a study of the development of the adolescent girl under primitive conditions. It was the first book of its kind that combined anthropological data and psychology. It was so interesting to read that it became popular not only among anthropologists but with the general public.

2. Curator and Professor

In 1926 Margaret Mead was appointed curator of ethnology at the American Museum of Natural History in New York. She maintained her association with the museum for fifty years.

She was also a professor of anthropology at Columbia, and she taught courses at several other universities as well. She helped found the anthropology departments at N.Y.U. in 1965 and Fordham's Liberal Arts College in 1968. She was associated with many professional organizations and was president of the American Anthropological Association.

3. Other Roles

Margaret was active in many causes and campaigns and worked in various ways to end world hunger. She helped establish UNESCO.

Besides her writings in anthropology, she also wrote about child psychology, cross-cultural communication, progressive education, family, male-female relationships, sex, and moral and religious issues. She was consulted on major social issues by educators, government leaders, and religious leaders. She received many honors and awards throughout her career. After years of battling cancer, she died in 1978.

Famous Women
of the Twentieth Century
Lisa F. DeWitt

Cue Cards

PRO LINGUA ● ASSOCIATES

Famous Women
of the Twentieth Century
Lisa F. DeWitt

Marian Anderson

On prejudice: "Sometimes, it's like a hair across your cheek. You can't see it, you can't find it with your fingers, but you keep brushing at it because the feel of it is irritating."

Born: February 17, 1902, in Philadelphia, Pennsylvania.

Education: High school graduate; voice training with various teachers.

Occupation: Opera singer, United Nations delegate.

Honors: Presidential Medal of Freedom — 1963; National Arts Hall of Fame — 1972; Kennedy Center Honor, Lifetime Achievement — 1978.

1. A voice "Once in a Hundred Years"

Marian Anderson started singing in her church choir when she was six years old and by the time she was in high school her beautiful, deep singing voice had developed and attracted the attention of a well-known black actor, John Thomas Butler. He sent her for serious vocal training, and later she studied at the Philadelphia Choral Society.

In 1925 Marian won a contest to sing in New York City. She sang beautifully, but because she was black it was not easy to find other singing engagements. She decided to study and tour in Europe and did very well. During a 1931 concert tour in Scandinavia she sang for Jan Sibelius, who honored her by dedicating his song "Solitude" to her.

Before she returned to America she sang at the Salzburg Festival, where Arturo Toscanini said to Marian, "Yours is a voice one hears once in a hundred years."

2. Back in America

On December 30, 1935, Marian gave a concert in New York City, and the New York *Times* said, "Marian Anderson has returned to her native land one of the greatest singers of our time."

Soon after, in 1936, the Roosevelts invited her to sing at the White House. Then three years later, three blocks from the White House at Constitution Hall, the Daughters of the American Revolution refused to permit her to sing there because she was black. To show her support, Eleanor Roosevelt resigned from the DAR. Later, on Easter Sunday in 1939, Eleanor Roosevelt arranged for Marian to sing from the steps of the Lincoln Memorial, where more than 75,000 people gathered to hear her.

On January 7, 1955, a seventy-two-year tradition was broken when Marian Anderson became the first black opera singer to sing with the Metropolitan Opera Company in New York City.

3. Honors

In 1957 she went on tour to Asia. The tour was sponsored by the United Nations. While she was in India she became the first foreigner to be invited to speak at the Mahatma Gandhi Memorial in Delhi, India.

When she returned, she was appointed by President Dwight D. Eisenhower as a delegate to the United Nations.

In 1959 she was elected to the American Academy of Arts and Sciences, and on December 6, 1963, she received the Presidential Medal of Freedom (the highest honor for a civilian).

As an official guest, she sang *The Star-Spangled Banner* at the Inauguration of President John F. Kennedy in 1961. Then on April 19, 1965, she sang her farewell concert at Carnegie Hall and retired from the music world.

Famous Women
of the Twentieth Century
Lisa F. DeWitt

Cue Cards

PRO LINGUA ● ASSOCIATES

Famous Women
of the Twentieth Century
Lisa F. DeWitt

Margaret Bourke-White

"Nothing attracts me like a closed door. I cannot let my camera rest until I have pried it open, and I wanted to be first."

Born: June 14, 1904, in New York City.

Died: August 27, 1971.

Education: Columbia University, University of Michigan, Cornell University (graduated in 1927).

Occupation: Photojournalist.

1. First Woman Photojournalist

Margaret Bourke-White was the first woman photojournalist. Her career as a photographer and editor for *Life* magazine lasted for thirty-three years.

It was Margaret who first saw the beauty and power in telling the story of American industry. She moved to Cleveland and began photographing its mines, mills, docks, factories, railroads, and bridges. Then in 1929, she moved to New York City to work for *Fortune* magazine.

2. Opening Doors

In 1930, Margaret traveled to the Soviet Union, which was a closed door. Margaret opened that door; her photographs were her passport. She took pictures and filmed the people, the factories, and Stalin's great-aunt and mother. The photographs were published in 1931 in her book, *Eyes on Russia*.

In 1936 she started working with *Life* magazine, and later that same year she worked with Southern writer Erskine Caldwell to produce *You Have Seen Their Faces*, a book about Southern sharecroppers. Margaret and Erskine were married from 1939 to 1942, and together they produced two more books.

3. War Correspondent

Life magazine made special arrangements with the Pentagon, and Margaret became the first woman war correspondent. The first uniform for a woman war correspondent was designed for her. After the start of WWII she flew to England and North Africa to cover troop action. She followed General Patton's Third Army during the final days of the war. Her photographs and text from that period were later published into one of her most famous books, *The Living Dead of Buchenwald*.

4. The Final Years

In 1946, *Life* magazine sent Margaret to India, where she photographed and filmed Mahatma Gandhi. She traveled to South Africa in 1950 to do a photo essay on its problems and its people. Margaret's last assignment was to cover the Korean conflict. She writes: "In a whole lifetime of taking pictures, a photographer knows that the time will come when he will take one picture that seems most important of all." This picture was the tender reunion of a Korean mother with the son she thought had died.

By the mid-1950s, her work had to end because of Parkinson's disease. Margaret fought courageously until her death. Margaret Bourke-White left behind a remarkable visual history of her times.

Cue Cards

**Famous Women
of the Twentieth Century
Lisa F. DeWitt**

PRO LINGUA ⬤ ASSOCIATES

**Famous Women
of the Twentieth Century
Lisa F. DeWitt**

Lillian Hellman

"I cannot and will not cut my conscience to fit this year's fashions."

Born: June 20, 1905, in New Orleans, Louisiana.

Died: June 30, 1984.

Education: Attended New York University and Columbia University.

Occupation: Playwright.

1. The Woman Playwright

Lillian Hellman was the first major female playwright and one of the most important of the 20th century. She set the Broadway stage for the exploration of the sexual, familial, and social issues that directly affect women's lives. She was a woman working in a male-dominated field and yet she managed to get financial backing for her plays. She was the boss when it came to producing one of her plays. She was a strong character — cynical, witty, critical, outspoken, and not well liked —but no one could dispute her genius.

2. Introduction to Theater and the Literary World

Lillian Florence Hellman was born into a Jewish family in New Orleans, Louisiana. She was an only child. She kept a journal about the people in her life. There were elderly, eccentric aunts, an absent father, and two black nannies.

She later attended New York University and Columbia University but did not graduate. She took a job as a manuscript reader, and later worked as a theatrical playreader in New York and as a scenario reader in Hollywood.

3. The Plays

In her late twenties, after her seven-year marriage to writer Arthur Kober, she began living with the well-known detective story-writer, Dashiell Hammett. Then in 1934 she wrote her first successful play, *The Children's Hour*, a tragedy of a malicious child accusing the owners of her boarding school of lesbianism. The play was a Broadway success. The late 1930s and 1940s were her most productive writing years, and her plays won many awards.

She also wrote the screenplays for three of her plays, which were made into Hollywood movies — *The Children's Hour*, *The Little Foxes*, and *The Searching Wind*.

4. Blacklisted

During and after World War II there was a strong anti-communism movement in the United States — the McCarthy era. Lillian and Dashiell Hammett had joined the Communist Party in the 1930s; she later withdrew, but he was sent to prison for six months because of his membership. They were among the many writers and actors in Hollywood that were blacklisted — prevented from continuing their work.

5. Memoirs

After the McCarthy era, Lillian wrote *Toys in the Attic* (1960) and three autobiographies. There was debate over the accuracy of her memoirs. The questions were to remain unanswered. Lillian Hellman died of a heart attack after years of heavy smoking and drinking. At her funeral a friend said: "She gave us this anger to remember and use in a bad world."

Famous Women
of the Twentieth Century
Lisa F. DeWitt

Cue Cards

PRO LINGUA  ASSOCIATES

Famous Women
of the Twentieth Century
Lisa F. DeWitt

Rachel Carson

"Man is a part of nature, and his war against nature is . . . a war against himself."

Born: May 27, 1907, in Springdale, Pennsylvania.

Died: April 14, 1964.

Education: B.A. in Science (1929) — Pennsylvania College for Women. M.A. in Marine Biology (1932) — Johns Hopkins University.

Occupation: Environmentalist, marine biologist, writer.

1. Interest in the Sea

As a young child, Rachel Carson longed to see the ocean. Instead, she spent many long hours outside, observing the animals in the meadows, creeks, and woods on her family's 65-acre farm. Even as a child she showed a reverence and fascination for all life.

In school Rachel loved science and enjoyed writing. By the age of ten she had published and been paid for her first story. When she went to college she made the difficult choice to major in biology instead of English. After she graduated at the top of her class, she was invited to do ocean research at Woods Hole in Massachusetts. After that, Johns Hopkins University in Baltimore, Maryland, offered her a full scholarship and she continued her ocean research.

2. Writing

In 1935 Rachel was hired as an aquatic biologist writer for the U.S. government. One part of her job was to write brochures. Her writing was often too poetic for the brochures so she started selling her articles to magazines.

In 1941 her first book, *Under the Sea Wind*, was published. It was about the Atlantic coastal sea floor and explained the interdependence of the sea plants and animals.

In 1950, *The Sea Around Us* was published. In it she introduced the concept that the earth, with its seas, is a balanced planet where nothing is ever wasted. Both of her books became best sellers.

She was very uncomfortable giving speeches but she traveled and spoke to thousands. She became known as the pioneer of ecology.

3. A Warning

Then in 1962, her most controversial and influential book, *Silent Spring*, was published. The book exposed the dangers of pesticides — particularly DDT. The government and the chemical companies told everyone that they were safe, but pesticides were making people and animals sick. The chemical companies and the Department of Agriculture argued with Rachel Carson. Finally, President John F. Kennedy asked for a special report from the top scientists to decide who was right. When the report came out it agreed with Rachel Carson's research. New laws were made to limit chemical pollution, and DDT was eventually completely banned.

Silent Spring was published in many different languages with her warning: "If we keep using these chemicals, spring might someday come silently with no birds left to sing, and no people left to hear them."

Cue Cards

**Famous Women
of the Twentieth Century
Lisa F. DeWitt**

PRO LINGUA ● ASSOCIATES

**Famous Women
of the Twentieth Century
Lisa F. DeWitt**

Sylvia Ashton-Warner

"When I teach people, I marry them."

Born: December 17, 1908, in Stratford, New Zealand.

Died: April 28, 1984.

Education: Graduated 1931 — Teacher's College, Auckland, New Zealand.

Occupation: Writer and educator.

1. A New Zealand School-teacher

Sylvia Ashton-Warner grew up in the small town of Stratford, New Zealand. After graduating from college she married a fellow student, Keith Henderson. Sylvia and her husband had three children and taught together in the remote schools for white and Maori (the native people) children in the North Island area of New Zealand until her husband's death in 1969.

During these years Sylvia began writing. She finished her first novel, *Spinster*, in 1959. It is about a New Zealand schoolteacher. The book became a bestseller in the United States and was made into a movie entitled *Two Loves*, starring Shirley MacLaine.

2. "Organic Teaching"

In 1963 Sylvia Ashton-Warner became an educator who profoundly influenced the education of young children around the world because of her book, *Teacher*. In this book she explains her method of "organic teaching" and how she used the language and the lives of the Maori children to lead them to their first reading, and to writing their own stories in their own books. "Only the organic style, the material coming from the mind of our child himself, wherever he is, whatever color he is, can accommodate him. Only his own clothes fit him."

3. An Influential Educator

For ten years Sylvia traveled, taught, and consulted with schools in India, Israel, England, and the United States.

She was a professor of education at an experimental school, Aspen Community School Teaching Center in Aspen, Colorado. In 1972 she wrote *Spearpoint: Teacher in America*. In it she wrote her conclusions about American society and how it affects children and their connection with life, with one another, with school and family — even with pets.

It was not until 1982, however, when she was made a member of the Order of the British Empire, that her position as one of the world's most influential educators was fully and officially recognized.

Famous Women
of the Twentieth Century
Lisa F. DeWitt

Cue Cards

PRO LINGUA  ASSOCIATES

Famous Women
of the Twentieth Century
Lisa F. DeWitt

Mother Teresa of Calcutta

"We can do no great things — only small things with great love."

Born: August 27, 1910, in Skopje, Yugoslavia.

Education: Order of the Sisters of Our Lady of Loreto.

Occupation: Nun and founder of the Missionaries of Charity.

Honors: Awarded the Nobel Peace Prize in 1979.

1. A Life of Service

Mother Teresa is internationally respected and loved for her work in relieving the sufferings of the poor, the abandoned, and the dying. She is a tireless worker and visits the people in her order's homes, hospitals, and orphanages daily.

In 1979 her life of service was internationally recognized when she was awarded the Nobel Peace Prize.

2. Service Around the World

In 1959 she founded a Roman Catholic order — the Missionaries of Charity — in Calcutta, India. Today Mother Teresa's order operates more than 430 homes in 95 countries to "help the poorest of the poor." There is even a home in New York City because, as Mother Teresa says, "you can find Calcutta all over the world."

In 1982, she helped evacuate mentally retarded children who had been forgotten during the height of battles between Israeli troops and the Palestine Liberation Organization in Beirut, Lebanon.

Wherever she goes in the world Mother Teresa serves God by "putting His love into action."

3. Beginnings in Calcutta

In 1948 Mother Teresa was granted special permission from the Vatican to leave her teaching position at the order of the Sisters of Our Lady of Loreto in Calcutta. Without companions, money, or a plan she left to work in the slums. She took off the dress of a Loreto nun and put on a cheap, simple, white sari with a blue border, a small cross pinned to the left shoulder, and open sandals on her feet. She began by picking up a dying man and taking him to a friend's home to die with dignity.

4. The Work Continues.

Every day people are picked up off the streets by the sisters and brothers of the Missionaries of Charity and taken to homes for the sick or dying, and children are taken to orphanages for adoption. The problems are great, and the work is endless, but Mother Teresa's message of love continues.

Famous Women
of the Twentieth Century
Lisa F. DeWitt

Cue Cards

PRO LINGUA ● ASSOCIATES

Famous Women
of the Twentieth Century
Lisa F. DeWitt

Copyright © 1993 by Pro Lingua Associates, Address: 15 Elm Street, Brattleboro, Vermont 05301 U.S.A. Telephone: 800-366-4775.

Sonja Henie

About skating: *"It's a sense of power, of command over distance and gravity, and an illusion of no longer having to move because movement is carrying you."*

Born: April 8, 1912, in Oslo, Norway.

Died: October 12, 1969.

Education: Private tutoring.

Occupation: Figure skater, movie actress.

Honors: Olympic gold medals in figure skating in 1928, 1932, 1936.

1. A Young Athlete

As a child growing up in Norway, Sonja Henie started skiing and skating at age five. She also studied ballet in the summers. When she turned six she got her first real pair of figure skates. At age nine she entered and won her first competition and then won again at age ten. Her family started taking her skating seriously, and her father helped her to train for the national championships.

2. Grace and Technique Combined

In 1923 Sonja became the national champion of Norway and in 1926 she came in second in the world championships. One year later in Oslo, she won her first world figure skating championship, and in 1928 she won the Olympic gold medal in figure skating. She attributed her success to intensive practice under her father's guidance and to the dancing of the famous Russian ballet dancer, Anna Pavlova. She had seen Anna dance in 1927. Sonja was the first figure skater to combine the grace of ballet with the strength and techniques of figure skating.

3. A Second Career

Sonja won two other Olympic gold medals, one in 1932 and the other in 1936. Then she decided to end her amateur career in skating and begin her new career in the movies. She starred in her first movie in 1936, *One in a Million*, about a skater's rise to fame. From 1937 to 1939 she made five more very successful movies. She was a very popular star of the time.

4. The Arts

In 1941 she became a U.S. citizen. In 1949, after two previous marriages, she married Niels Onstad, a wealthy Norwegian ship owner. In 1968 she and her husband opened a center for the visual and performing arts outside of Oslo. Fourteen months later she died of leukemia.

Famous Women
of the Twentieth Century
Lisa F. DeWitt

Cue Cards

PRO LINGUA ◖ ASSOCIATES

Famous Women
of the Twentieth Century
Lisa F. DeWitt

Mildred ("Babe") Didrikson Zaharias

"I don't seem able to do my best unless I'm behind or in trouble."

Born: June 26, 1914, in Port Arthur, Texas.

Died: September 27, 1956.

Education: High school graduate.

Occupation: Sportswoman; amateur and professional golfer.

Honors: Outstanding Woman Athlete of the Century (1949 Associated Press Poll).

1. Youth

Mildred Ella Didrikson is noted as one of the greatest and most versatile women in sports. When she was a child in Port Arthur, Texas, she was an avid baseball player and was nicknamed "Babe" after the famous American baseball player, Babe Ruth. She played basketball in high school and semipro basketball with the Texas Cyclones. She led the team to a national championship.

2. The Olympics

In 1932, "Babe" competed in the Olympics, and won gold medals for the 80-meter hurdles and the javelin throw and a silver medal for the high jump. Later that same year, she played professional basketball for the Babe Didrikson All-American Basketball Team.

3. Golf

She turned to playing golf, and after she won the Texas Women's Amateur Golf Championship in 1935, she became a professional golfer. By 1946 "Babe" had become the only three-time winner of the Associated Press Woman Athlete of the Year Award. She then went on to win the award three more times. She was one of the founders of the Ladies' Professional Golf Association, formed in 1948, and in 1949 she won 17 straight golf tournaments.

She married George Zaharias, a wrestler, in 1938.

4. Final Years

In 1954, even though she was very ill with colon cancer, she won the U.S. Women's Open golf title for the third time. She seemed indestructible, but died only two years later in Galveston, Texas.

Famous Women
of the Twentieth Century
Lisa F. DeWitt

Cue Cards

PRO LINGUA ● ASSOCIATES

Famous Women
of the Twentieth Century
Lisa F. DeWitt

Indira Gandhi

In her will: "No hate is dark enough to overshadow the extent of my love for my people and my country."

Born: November 19, 1917, in Allahabad, India.

Died: October 31, 1984.

Education: Boarding schools in India and Switzerland; attended Oxford University in England.

Occupation: Prime Minister of India for 18 years.

1. The Early Years

Indira Nehru Gandhi was born into a wealthy Brahmin political family on November 19, 1917, in Allahabad in northern India. Her father, Jawaharlal Nehru, ruled India as its prime minister for the first 17 years after its independence from British rule in 1947.

After her schooling abroad she returned to India, in 1941.

She joined her father's National Congress Party, which led the fight for India's independence. She married a lawyer, Feroze Gandhi, in 1942 and had two sons, Rajiv and Sanjay.

2. Preparation for Politics

Her mother died in 1936, and during her father's rule, Indira served as her widowed father's official hostess and confidante at political gatherings.

In 1955 she was elected to the working committee of the Congress Party. Then in 1959 she was elected the party's president. In her first 11 months as President she showed the toughness and strength for which she was to be known throughout her political career.

3. Prime Minister of India

Her father died in 1964. She became Prime Minister of India on January 24, 1966. She held this position for almost two decades, excluding the three years from 1977 to 1980.

Indira Gandhi was loved and admired but also hated. She was often called "the world's most powerful woman." She was talented in foreign affairs and became an ally of the Soviet Union, which later helped India win the war with Pakistan in 1971, creating independent Bangladesh.

4. Assassination

On the morning of October 31, 1984, as she walked through the garden at her home and office in New Delhi, she was assassinated by Beant Singh, who had been a member of her bodyguard for nine years, and a police constable, Satwant Singh, both members of a militant Sikh sect.

The assassination was a retaliation by militant Sikhs who were angered by the Indian army's attack on the Sikhs' holiest shrine — the Golden Temple at Amritsar — in June 1984.

Her younger son, Sanjay, whom she had prepared to succeed her, died in a plane crash in 1980. So it was her elder son, Rajiv, who was sworn in as the new Prime Minister late on October 31.

Famous Women
of the Twentieth Century
Lisa F. DeWitt

Cue Cards

PRO LINGUA ● ASSOCIATES

Famous Women
of the Twentieth Century
Lisa F. DeWitt

Eva Perón

"Without fanaticism one cannot accomplish anything."

Born: May 7, 1919, in Los Toldos, Argentina.

Died: July 26, 1952.

Education: Two years of high school.

Occupation: First Lady of Argentina 1946-1952.

1. Eva María Duarte

Eva María was the youngest of five illegitimate children born to Juana Ibarguren, the mistress of Juan Duarte, in the small village of Los Toldos, Argentina. Her father left when Eva was six years old, and to support the family her mother sewed clothes for people in the village.

At a young age Eva knew that she wanted to be a famous actress. She was fifteen when she finally arrived in Buenos Aires to work in radio. There are not many details about her early life; even in her autobiography — *La razón de mi vida* — there is no mention of childhood occurrences or dates.

2. Meeting Perón

On January 16, 1944, there was an earthquake in Argentina that destroyed the town of San Juan. In Buenos Aires a collection on behalf of the survivors began. The San Juan Fund was organized by the Secretary of Labor in the military government, Colonel Juan Domingo Perón. It was his idea to have an "artistic festival" at which actors and members of the armed forces would march through the streets collecting money for San Juan. And so Eva Duarte met Juan Perón.

3. The Peróns

Juan and Eva were married on October 21, 1945. Juan Perón was inaugurated as President of Argentina on June 4, 1946. Eva had campaigned hard for his election, and his victory was also her victory. She was not only a First Lady but also served in the Ministry of Labor and gained the support of the working classes. Eva distributed food, money, and clothing to the poor. She came to be affectionately called "Evita." By June 1947, she had established her own welfare foundation that had an annual income of $100 million. With this money she sponsored homes for working girls, poor mothers, and the aged. She built hospitals and homes, gave personal loans and scholarships, and provided free legal aid to the poor. Evita was also the guiding spirit in the women's right to vote movement. The right was achieved in September 1947.

She formed the Peronista Women's Party and traveled abroad to spread Peronism. She considered running for Vice President of Argentina, but instead concentrated on helping her husband. He was reelected for a second six-year term on November 11, 1951. Although Evita was severely ill with uterine cancer, she lived to see her husband inaugurated on June 4, 1952. She died one month later.

4. Evita

There are still many unanswered questions about the Perón regime and Juan and Evita. But the name "Evita" still evokes the picture of a politically powerful, beautiful, ambitious, and ruthless woman who had many titles, including "Lady of Hope" and "Mother of the Innocents."

**Famous Women
of the Twentieth Century
Lisa F. DeWitt**

Cue Cards

PRO LINGUA  ASSOCIATES

**Famous Women
of the Twentieth Century
Lisa F. DeWitt**

Nadine Gordimer

"It is possible to opt out of class and color. . . . You can be a part of the new South Africa."

Born: November 20, 1923. in Springs, South Africa.

Education: Attended private schools and the University of Witwatersrand.

Occupation: Writer.

Honors: Many literary awards, including the Nobel Prize in Literature, 1991.

Publications: More than 200 short stories, 9 collections of short stories, and ten novels.

1. Apartheid

Nadine Gordimer was born and raised in the segregated town of Springs outside of Johannesburg, South Africa. Her parents were Jewish immigrants from London, England, and her childhood was typically middle-class. Her political awareness developed gradually, but in time she realized that the oppression of the blacks in South Africa was a man-made, not a God-given, right. For almost 40 years she has spoken out against apartheid — the laws and restrictions that enable the white minority to control and suppress the country's black majority.

2. The Nobel Prize

In October 1991, Nadine Gordimer was honored when she became the first woman in 25 years and the first South African to win the Nobel Prize in Literature. Archbishop Desmond Tutu, who won the Nobel Peace Prize in 1984, says that the prize is "a tremendous acknowledgement of an outstanding stalwart against injustice and oppression. And it couldn't have happened to a nicer person."

She said that it was the second thrill in her life in two years, the first being the release of Nelson Mandela from prison. She planned to use some of the money to support the new Department of Arts and Culture of the African National Congress.

3. Writing

Even though Nadine is a member of the ANC (African National Congress) she says that this has nothing to do with her writing and that she will not use her writing as propaganda. She has no illusions about the virtue of the oppressed, only the need to end the oppression.

At one time three of her books were banned, but under political reforms, they have become available. Nadine Gordimer continues to write and says that every time she finishes a book she thinks she is done, that she has said all she has to say; then she goes on living, but something else comes up, and she must say it.

Cue Cards

**Famous Women
of the Twentieth Century
Lisa F. DeWitt**

PRO LINGUA ASSOCIATES

**Famous Women
of the Twentieth Century
Lisa F. DeWitt**

Shirley Chisholm

"Of my two 'handicaps,' being female put many more obstacles in my path than being black."

Born: November 30, 1924, in Brooklyn, New York.

Education: B.A., Sociology, Brooklyn College, 1945. M.A., Education, Columbia University, 1947.

Occupation: Congresswoman and teacher.

Honors: First black woman to be elected to Congress — 1968. More than thirty honorary degrees.

Publications: *Unbought and Unbossed* (autobiography) — 1970. *The Good Fight* — 1973.

1. Preparation

Shirley Chisholm was born in Brooklyn, New York, but she was raised by her grandmother in Barbados. She was brought up with discipline and a Christian education, which she credits for her later successes. She learned at a young age to work hard and to feel proud of a job well done. She learned to read at three and a half and was writing at age four.

When she returned to the United States, she graduated from high school in New York City. She then entered Brooklyn College, and later she attended Columbia University. On October 8, 1949, she married Conrad Q. Chisholm, a Jamaican. She worked as the director of the Hamilton-Madison Child Care Center in New York City until 1959. Her experiences there led her to become involved in local politics.

2. Many Firsts

In 1964 she was elected to the State Assembly representing Brooklyn; she was the first black woman to represent that district. She won again in 1965 and 1966 and worked for the passing of various education bills.

In 1968, she won a seat in the U.S. House of Representatives from the twelfth district, which was mostly Democratic, Puerto Rican, and black. She was the first black woman to be elected to Congress, where she served until 1983. As a Congresswoman she worked hard for federal aid to state welfare departments, and she spoke out in favor of women in politics.

In 1971 she was appointed to the House Education and Labor Committee, and in 1972 she ran for the Democratic nomination for President of the United States. She campaigned long and hard and even though she didn't win the nomination, she won the admiration and respect of fellow politicians, women, and black Americans.

3. Spokesperson

During her years in politics she was identified as a spokesperson for the needs of minorities, the poor, and the undereducated. Shirley Chisholm broke down the barriers in the world of politics that had existed for women and other minorities. She announced her retirement from public office in February 1982 and began teaching in 1983 at Mount Holyoke College in Massachusetts. She continues to write articles about her concerns.

Famous Women
of the Twentieth Century
Lisa F. DeWitt

Cue Cards

PRO LINGUA  ASSOCIATES

Famous Women
of the Twentieth Century
Lisa F. DeWitt

Margaret Thatcher

"I am extraordinarily patient, provided I get my own way in the end."

Born: October 13, 1925, in Grantham, England.

Education: B.S., Chemistry, Somerville College at Oxford University, 1947. M.A., Oxford University, 1950.

Occupation: Prime Minister of England, 1979-1990.

Honors: Order of Merit — given to her by Queen Elizabeth II on December 7, 1990.

1. Humble Beginnings

Margaret Hilda Roberts was born into a lower middle-class family in Grantham, England. Her father was a Methodist minister and local politician, her mother a dressmaker. As a child, Margaret would go with her father to local political meetings. Her father had high expectations of Margaret and saw that she was ambitious. So, even though the family had no money for indoor plumbing or hot water in their apartment above a grocery store, her father sent Margaret to a good local grammar school and paid for tutoring in the classics so that she could meet the requirements to enter Oxford University. She also took elocution lessons to improve her accent.

2. Coming Into Her Own

While at Somerville College at Oxford University, she majored in chemistry and joined the Oxford University Conservative Association. She was elected its first female president. She excelled in political debating at Oxford and later became involved in local Tory politics. In 1947, after she graduated with a degree in chemistry, she began working as a research chemist.

In 1950 she ran for a seat in Parliament. She was the youngest person to run, and although she lost, she ran again the following year and increased her support.

She married Denis Thatcher, a wealthy businessman, in 1951 and gave birth to twins in 1953. Four months later she passed her bar exam and practiced patent law until 1961.

3. As Prime Minister

From 1961 until 1975 she was a member of Parliament, and in February 1975 she became the first woman to head the Conservative Party. She became Britain's first woman Prime Minister in May 1979; in June 1983 she was elected to a second term.

Then in June 1987 she was elected to a third term, but on November 22, 1990, she announced that she would resign after she failed to win re-election as Conservative Party Leader.

Her 11 years and 29 weeks in office was the fifth longest consecutive term in British history and the longest in the 20th century.

4. Iron Lady

The term "Iron Lady" was given to her by the Soviet press after she strongly denounced communism in 1976. But she was also called "Iron Lady" because of her strong will and skill in argument and debate. She has a domineering personality and has been compared to Winston Churchill, Queen Elizabeth I, and Queen Victoria.

Famous Women
of the Twentieth Century
Lisa F. DeWitt

Cue Cards

PRO LINGUA ● ASSOCIATES

Famous Women
of the Twentieth Century
Lisa F. DeWitt

Elisabeth Kübler-Ross

"It's only when we truly know and understand that we have a limited time on earth — and that we have no way of knowing when our time is up — that we will begin to live each day to the fullest, as if it was the only one we had."

Born: July 8, 1926, in Zurich, Switzerland.

Education: M.D., University of Zurich, 1957.

Occupation: Psychiatrist, thanatologist, and writer.

1. Identity

Elisabeth Kübler was born in Zurich, Switzerland, the first of a set of triplets. Growing up, she felt that she had no identity, being one of three children whose parents couldn't tell them apart. She said that this experience was necessary for her later work with multi-handicapped children who had no identity; they were only numbers in an institution. She became determined, as a doctor, to know each of her patients individually.

2. Finding Her Profession

During WWII, Elisabeth volunteered at the Kantonsspital, Zurich's largest hospital. She helped thousands of refugees who had fled from Nazi Germany. After the war she traveled throughout Europe, working as a cook, mason and roofer. She also helped to open typhoid and first aid stations. She visited Majdanek, one of the concentration camps in Poland, where an estimated 960,000 had been killed in the gas chambers. This visit changed her life; she knew that she wanted to study medicine.

She returned to Switzerland and entered the University of Zurich. She received her M.D. degree in 1957 and in 1958 married a fellow medical student, Emanuel Robert Ross.

She did her internship in New York City and later accepted a fellowship in psychiatry at the Psychopathic Hospital at the University of Colorado School of Medicine in Denver. She taught psychiatry and psychophysiology at the University's Colorado General Hospital.

In 1965 she became assistant professor of psychiatry at the University of Chicago Medical School. While there she began the work that later made her famous.

3. Thanatology — The Study of Death

Dr. Kübler-Ross began teaching her medical students how to talk with terminally ill patients. She had learned that dying patients want to be able to talk about what is happening to them.

She discussed her research and work in her first book, *On Death and Dying*, (1969). The book became a bestseller and is also a reference work for those in the counseling professions. Today, courses on the art of helping people deal with death are included in the curriculum of all medical, nursing, social work, and theological schools; programs on aspects of death are offered at universities, hospitals, and schools.

4. Butterflies — What Death Is All About

Twenty-five years after she visited Majdanek, where she observed butterflies scratched into the wooden barrack walls by children going to the gas chambers, she observed that her dying children patients always draw butterflies. Her conclusion is that "Dying is nothing else but a butterfly coming out of a cocoon. That's what death is all about."

Famous Women
of the Twentieth Century
Lisa F. DeWitt

Cue Cards

PRO LINGUA ● ASSOCIATES

Famous Women
of the Twentieth Century
Lisa F. DeWitt

Barbara Walters

"To sacrifice friends, love, and a view of the sunset, no matter how occasional, all for a career simply isn't worth it."

Born: September 25, 1931, in Brookline, Massachusetts.

Education: B.A., Sarah Lawrence College, 1954.

Occupation: Television news reporter, interviewer, writer, correspondent, and producer.

Honors: 1974 Woman of the Year in Communications; 1975 Broadcaster of the Year; 1975 Emmy Award.

1. A Genius at Interviewing

Barbara Walters is best known for her in-depth, entertaining TV interviews with world leaders and celebrities. She has a particular genius for getting people she is interviewing to reveal who they really are behind their public faces.

2. From Writer to Co-host

She began her television career at WRCA-TV in New York City and eventually became a producer and writer. She later worked for CBS-TV as a writer for the morning news. In 1961 she was hired to write for the NBC *"Today"* show. Barbara was not in front of the camera until 1965, when she filled a temporary position on *"Today."* By 1974 she was a regular co-host of the show.

3. First Woman of Evening News

In 1976, she became the first woman to anchor an evening network newscast, on ABC-TV. She also became the highest paid on-air reporter when she signed a $1 million dollar contract with ABC-TV. Barbara is quoted as saying, "Most men realize to get the big job, they often have to hang in there and do the grubby ones. Many women, especially those who do not have to work, do not know this. I hung in there."

4. The Million-dollar Contract

The $1 million contract can be seen as an acknowledgement of the valuable contributions of Barbara Walters, but also as an acknowledgement of the important role of women in television news. Serious news was no longer just a man's job to report. Barbara continues to report and interview and is currently a co-host on ABC's sixty-minute news program, *20/20*.

**Famous Women
of the Twentieth Century
Lisa F. DeWitt**

Cue Cards

PRO LINGUA ◑ ASSOCIATES

**Famous Women
of the Twentieth Century
Lisa F. DeWitt**

Dian Fossey

". . . the next two decades are estimated to see the extinction of twenty species of animals. Human beings must decide whether or not the mountain gorilla will become one of them."

Born: January 16, 1932, in San Francisco, California.

Died: December 27, 1985.

Education: B.A., San Jose College, 1954.

Occupation: Conservationist and field researcher.

Publications: *Gorillas in the Mist* — 1983 (produced as a movie in 1988).

1. Life's Longing

In 1966, Dian Fossey left her ten-year job as an occupational therapist to begin the next eighteen years of her life living in the Vironga Mountains with mountain gorillas. She had always loved animals and had wanted to work with them, but she did not qualify for veterinary school. Occupational therapy was her second choice, because she also loved children. However, after she went on safari to Africa in 1963, she knew what she wanted to do for the next phase of her life.

2. Getting Started

British anthropologist Louis B. Leakey in Tanzania and Dr. Jane Goodall, the British specialist on chimpanzees, encouraged Fossey to study mountain gorillas. In 1967 she set up the Karisoke Research Center in Rwanda. She identified fifty-one gorillas living in four distinct family groups. She learned that these enormous animals, some weighing over 400 pounds and over six feet tall, were vegetarians and peaceful in their behavior. She also observed that they had a language — a system of sounds. The gorillas learned to accept and trust her and include her as part of their family.

3. "Nyiramachabelli"

For most of the eighteen years of field research, Dian worked alone from her base camp 10,000 feet above sea level, in torrential rains, hail, fog, and foot-deep mud. She fought off poachers, stole their traps, and dealt with government interference. The Africans named her "Nyiramachabelli," which means "the old lady who lives in the forest without a man," and many feared her.

Dian made many enemies in attempting to preserve the land and life of the mountain gorillas. She also made many friends around the world when she traveled to raise people's awareness of the plight of the rain forests and the mountain gorillas.

4. Final Years

In 1977, poachers killed Digit, a male gorilla who was extremely intelligent and special to Fossey. After this, Dian became even more enraged. In the remaining eight years there were many other sacrifices and hardships.

Then on December 27, 1985, Dian Fossey was found murdered in her cabin. Neither the identity of the murderer nor the motive has ever been determined. Dian Fossey is buried among the graves of her beloved gorillas next to Digit.

Famous Women
of the Twentieth Century
Lisa F. DeWitt

Cue Cards

PRO LINGUA ○ ASSOCIATES

Famous Women
of the Twentieth Century
Lisa F. DeWitt

Gloria Steinem

"Feminism is the belief that women are full human beings; it's simple justice."

Born: March 25, 1934, in Toledo, Ohio.

Education: B.A., Smith College, 1956.

Occupation: Writer, lecturer, editor and co-founder of *Ms.* magazine.

1. Gloria Steinem = Women's Liberation

Gloria Steinem's name is synonymous with the women's liberation movement. She has been a dedicated writer, speaker, and leader in the cause of equal rights for women for 30 years.

2. From Playboy Bunny to *Ms.*

Early in her career she was a Playboy bunny for one month at the Playboy Club in New York. She wrote an honest account of the world of the Playboy hostess and exposed what sexism in the workplace was all about. Since then, her articles have appeared in many national magazines. In 1972 she co-founded *Ms.* magazine. In this same year the U.S. Government Printing Office accepted the title *"Ms."* for use in federal forms and publications.

3. Women's Organizations

Gloria, along with Shirley Chisholm, the first black woman to be elected to Congress (1968-1982), and Bella Abzug, a N.Y. Congresswoman (1971-1977), formed the National Women's Political Caucus. She was also founder and board member of the Women's Action Alliance and the Coalition of Labor Union Women.

4. The ERA

In 1923 the Equal Rights Amendment was originated by Alice Paul. Almost 60 years later, Gloria Steinem, along with thousands of other women, supported and worked for its ratification. She was a tireless supporter, but in spite of all this support the amendment failed to be ratified and died on June 30, 1982. Gloria was named Woman of the Year by *McCall's* magazine in 1972 and continues to be noted on lists of the nation's most admired women.

**Famous Women
of the Twentieth Century
Lisa F. DeWitt**

Cue Cards

PRO LINGUA ● ASSOCIATES

**Famous Women
of the Twentieth Century
Lisa F. DeWitt**

Alice Walker

"Books are byproducts of our lives, deliver me from writers who say the way they live doesn't matter. I'm not sure a bad person can write a good book. If art doesn't make us better, then what on earth is it for?"

Born: February 9, 1944, in Eatonton, Georgia.

Education: Attended Spelman College; 1965 graduate of Sarah Lawrence College.

Occupation: Writer.

1. From Georgia to Africa and Back

Alice Malsenoir Walker was the youngest of eight children of a sharecropper father and a mother who worked as a maid. They lived in poverty, but Alice excelled in school and from the age of eight wrote her thoughts and poems in a notebook. When she was eight she had an accident that left her blind in her right eye.

This handicap did not affect her studies. She graduated from high school as valedictorian, and was offered a scholarship to Spelman, a black women's college in Atlanta, Georgia. She later transferred to Sarah Lawrence College in New York on another scholarship, traveled to Africa, and worked in the civil rights movement in Mississippi. It was there that she met and married Mel Leventhal, a civil rights lawyer. They had one child, Rebecca, and after ten years the couple divorced. Alice Walker continued to write and publish. In 1974, she joined the staff of *Ms.* magazine as contributing editor.

2. Successful Novelist

In her first novel, *The Third Life of Granger Copeland* (1970), she exposed violence against women, years before society had begun to tell the true story of abused women and domestic violence.

Meridian (1976), her second novel, about the civil rights movement and is used as a primary text in college American history and literature courses.

It was her third novel, *The Color Purple* (1982), that made Alice Walker popular. The book received the American Book Award and the Pulitzer Prize. In 1985, the book was made into a successful movie starring Whoopi Goldberg as its main character, Celie. Both the delicate and the brutal qualities of women's lives are explored, but friendship, love, and reliance among women triumphs.

3. A "Womanist"

Alice Walker is best known for her "womanist" theme. She prefers this term to "feminist" and explains that "womanist is to feminist as purple to lavender." Her characters are almost always Southern black women and yet they speak of universal female experience.

Famous Women
of the Twentieth Century
Lisa F. DeWitt

Cue Cards
PRO LINGUA  ASSOCIATES

Famous Women
of the Twentieth Century
Lisa F. DeWitt

Aung San Suu Kyi

"Democracy is the only ideology which is consistent with freedom."

Born: June 19, 1945, in Rangoon, Burma — now Myanmar.

Education: B.A., St. Hugh's College of Oxford University, 1967.

Occupation: Human rights activist and writer.

Honors: 1990 Sakharov Prize for Freedom of Thought. 1991 Nobel Peace Prize.

1. The Legacy of Aung San

Aung San Suu Kyi, whose name means "a bright collection of strange victories," was born in Rangoon, the capital of Burma. She was the youngest of three children. Her father, Aung San, led the Burmese nationalist movement in the 1940s. In 1948, Burma attained its independence after more than half a century of British rule and three years of Japanese occupation. Less than six months before Burma's independence, on July 19, 1947, Aung San was assassinated. Although Aung San Suu Kyi never knew her father, she was greatly influenced by him.

2. Transitions

In 1960 Aung San Suu Kyi left Burma with her mother to live in New Delhi, India. She attended an exclusive school also attended by Indira Gandhi's son Rajiv, who became Prime Minister of India. While in India, Aung San Suu Kyi learned about the teachings of Mohandas K. Gandhi, who taught and practiced nonviolent civil disobedience.

In 1972, she married Michael Aris, a scholar of Tibetan civilization, and worked for a short time as a research assistant at the United Nations in New York City. In 1973 the couple returned to England and had a son, Alexander, and four years later another son, Kim.

3. Return to Burma

While Aung San Suu Kyi was doing research on a book that she was writing about her father, her sense of responsibility to Burma resurfaced. The book about her father, *Aung San*, was published in 1984.

Then in April 1988, Aung San Suu Kyi returned to Rangoon to help care for her dying mother.

General Ne Win had ruled Burma since leading a military coup in 1962. Resistance to his rule climaxed in the summer of 1988. Protesters took to the streets of Rangoon, and thousands were killed August 8-13, when Ne Win's army fired into the crowds.

4. Involvement

Aung San Suu Kyi spoke to the crowds on August 26, standing before the Burma's most sacred shrine. With her people's support, she became the leader of the pro-democracy movement, traveling throughout Burma urging people not to give up their fight for freedom.

On July 20, 1989, she was placed under house arrest and forbidden to see her family.

5. The Nobel Prize

Aung San Suu Kyi was awarded the Nobel Peace Prize in 1991. The citation reads that she has become "one of the most extraordinary examples of civil courage in Asia in recent decades."

She is still under house arrest. The government has offered to set her free if she will leave her country forever, but she says she will stay and fight until Burma is free and democratic again.

Famous Women
of the Twentieth Century
Lisa F. DeWitt

Cue Cards
PRO LINGUA ● ASSOCIATES

Famous Women
of the Twentieth Century
Lisa F. DeWitt

Joan Benoit Samuelson

"My running has taught me that I can reach any goal if I want it enough."

Born: May 16, 1957, in Portland, Maine.

Education: 1980 graduate — Bowdoin College.

Occupation: Marathon runner, athlete.

Honors: Olympics 1984 — First woman to win the gold medal in the first-ever Olympic marathon for women.

1. Love of Sports

Joan Benoit grew up in the seacoast town of Cape Elizabeth, Maine, with three brothers. In her early years she learned how to keep up with them and compete. She exhibited ability in skiing, tennis, and field hockey while she was in school. When she was fifteen her dream was to be a member of the Olympic ski team, but her dream was shattered when she broke her leg skiing, so she began long-distance running. She continued training and competing through her college years.

2. Olympics

In 1979 Joan set an American record for the women's marathon, a twenty-six-mile course, when she won the Boston Marathon with a time of 2:35:15. She won again in 1983, setting a world's record with her time of 2:22:43.

Then in the 1984 Summer Olympic Games in Los Angeles, the women's marathon event was included for the first time. Joan's years of training and determination came together. Millions watched on television as she ran alone, ahead of all others, and entered the tunnel leading into the Los Angeles Coliseum where 77,000 spectators cheered. Her quiet life as a long-distance runner ended when she became the first woman to win the marathon event.

3. A New Goal

On September 29, 1984, Joan married Scott Samuelson, whom she had met at Bowdoin College. They live in Freeport, Maine, with their two children, Abigail and Anders. Joan continues to train and struggles to balance running, promotional work for Nike, being a spokesperson for various causes, and family responsibilities.

In her autobiography, *Running Tide* (1987), she writes that she won't quit running marathons until she can run one in 2:20 or less. In 1985, she almost reached her goal when she won the women's division of the America's Marathon in Chicago, setting a personal best of 2:21:21.

In the 1991 Boston Marathon Joan placed fourth; in the 1992 New York Marathon, sixth. Even if she never attains her sub-2:20 goal she will always be considered one of the greatest woman runners in U.S. history.

Famous Women
of the Twentieth Century
Lisa F. DeWitt

Cue Cards

PRO LINGUA ● ASSOCIATES

Famous Women
of the Twentieth Century
Lisa F. DeWitt

Rigoberta Menchú

"The horrors I have suffered are enough for me. And I've also felt in the deepest part of me what discrimination is, what exploitation is. It is the story of my life."

Born: 1959 in Chimel, Guatemala.

Education: None — taught herself how to read and write in Spanish at age 20.

Occupation: Guatemalan Indian rights activist, migrant farm worker, maid.

Honors: 1992 Nobel Peace Prize.

1. A Quiché Indian

Rigoberta Menchú is a Quiché Indian. She was born in the mountain village of Chimel, Guatemala. Her family, like many other Quiché Indian families, was very poor. At the age of eight she began working as a migrant farm worker with her parents and ten siblings.

2. Persecution

Her father, Vincente Menchú, started to unite other peasants, *los compañeros*, to resist the domination of wealthy landowners of Spanish and European descent. In January 1980, Vincente and other *compañeros* occupied the Spanish Embassy in Guatemala City to voice injustices. Police troops stormed into the embassy, a fire broke out, and Vincente and 38 others died.

Because of her father's politics the entire Menchú family has been persecuted. Rigoberta's mother and youngest brother were both kidnapped by Guatemalan soldiers and brutally tortured and killed. Today, she knows the whereabouts of only three of her sisters and one brother.

More than 120,000 people have "disappeared" and been openly murdered in the 30-year rebellion against Guatemala's repressive governments. The Guatemalan military is blamed for more than 50,000 deaths, mostly highland Indians, during the 1980s alone.

3. International Recognition

In 1981, after her mother's death, Rigoberta fled to Mexico. The Venezuelan writer Elisabeth Burgos-Deloray helped her write her story, *I, Rigoberta Menchú: An Indian Woman in Guatemala*, which was published in 1983. Her book tells of the Quiché Indians who make up about 60% of the population of Guatemala. It also tells of the large-scale repression of the Indians, and the torture and death of her family. The book has been translated into 11 languages, and Rigoberta has gained international recognition.

4. The Nobel Prize

Today, Rigoberta lives in one of Mexico City's poorest neighborhoods with other Guatemalan refugees. She was awarded the 1992 Nobel Peace Prize "in recognition of her work for social justice and ethno-cultural reconciliation." She will use the $1.2 million to set up a human rights foundation in her father's name. She says: "The only thing I wish for is freedom for Indians wherever they are. . . . As the end of the 20th century approaches, we hope that our continent will be pluralistic."

Famous Women
of the Twentieth Century
Lisa F. DeWitt

Cue Cards

PRO LINGUA ● ASSOCIATES

Famous Women
of the Twentieth Century
Lisa F. DeWitt